ACTIVITY BOOK 2

NATIONAL GEOGRAPHIC LEARNING

WELCOME TO OUR WORLD

SERIES EDITORS
JOAN KANG SHIN & JOANN (JODI) CRANDALL

NATIONAL GEOGRAPHIC LEARNING | CENGAGE Learning

Australia • Brazil • Mexico • Singapore • United Kingdom • United States

CAN YOU HELP ME?

1 LISTEN AND SAY. LISTEN AND CIRCLE. TR: 2

2 LISTEN AND COLOR. TR: 3

1 TABLE, SCISSORS, CRAYONS

1 SAY AND MATCH.

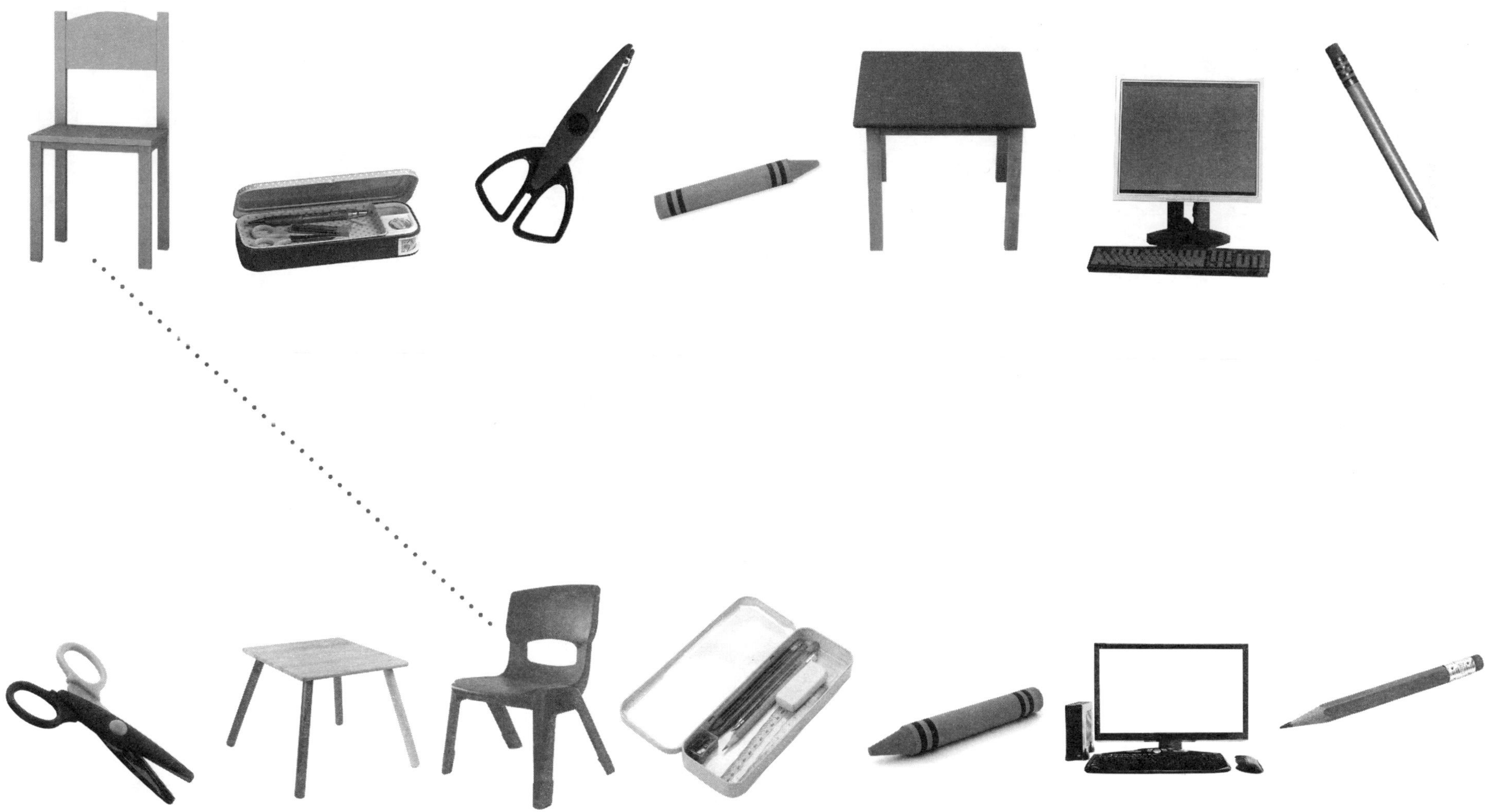

2 LISTEN AND CIRCLE. SAY. TR: 4

3 LISTEN AND SAY. CIRCLE. TR: 5

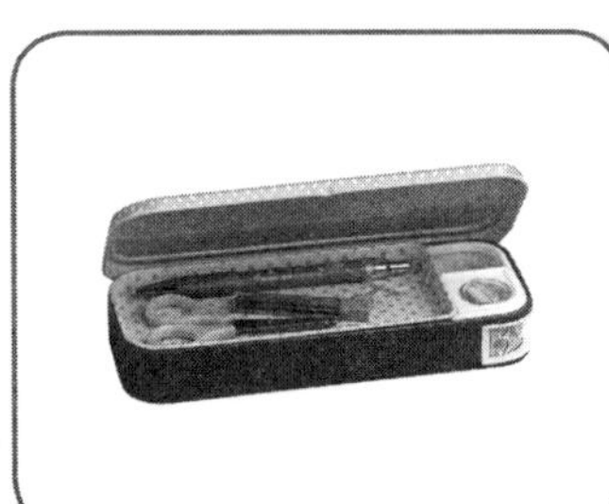

4 SAY AND MATCH.

IN

ON

UNDER

5 TRACE AND DRAW. SAY.

2 LET'S PLAY

1 SAY. FIND AND CIRCLE.

2 LISTEN AND CIRCLE. SAY. TR: 6

3 LISTEN AND SAY. CIRCLE. TR: 7

4 LOOK AND SAY *UP* OR *DOWN*. CIRCLE.

↓ ↑

↓ ↑

↓ ↑

↓ ↑

5 TRACE AND SAY.

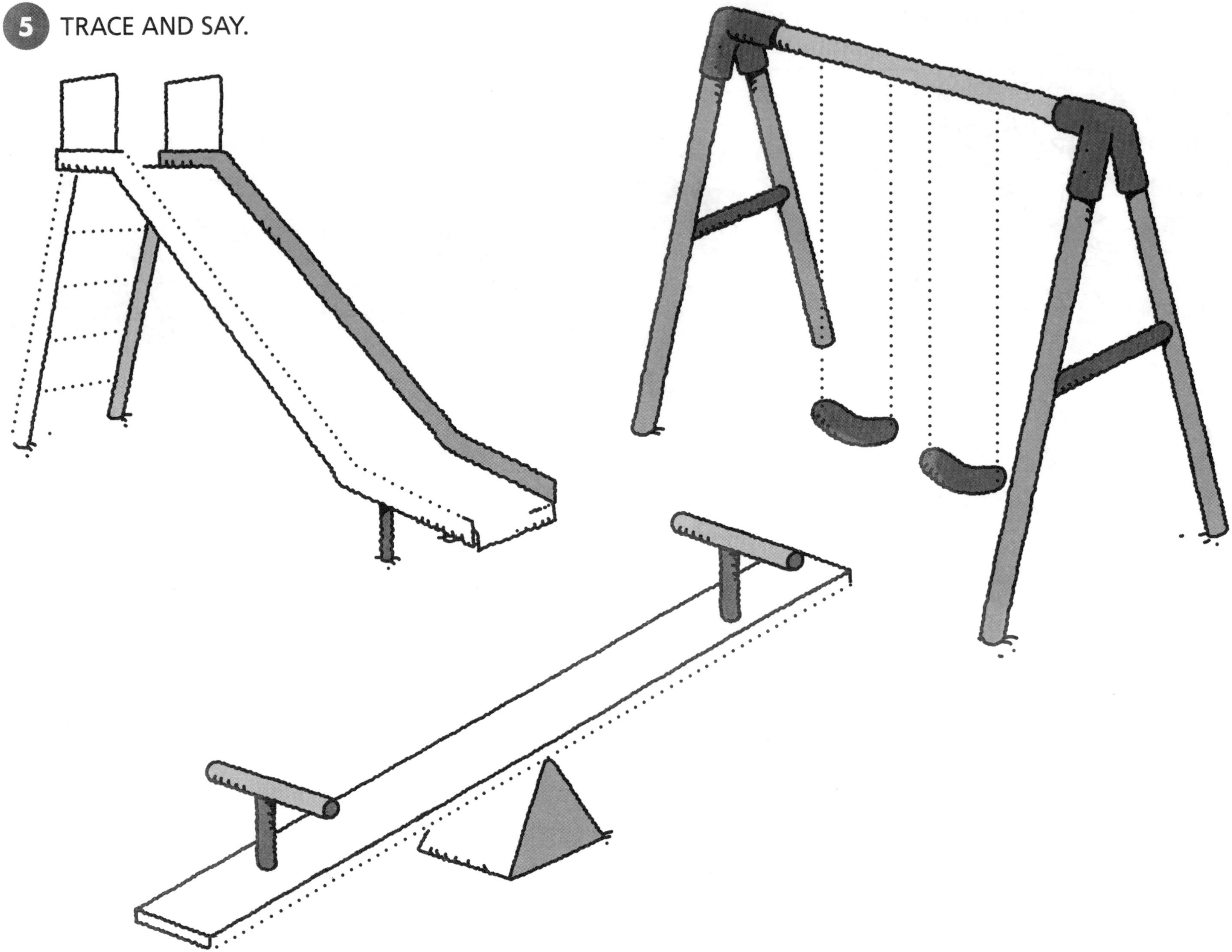

3 I LIKE RICE

1 LISTEN AND CIRCLE. SAY. TR: 8

2 LISTEN AND MATCH. TR: 9

1 2 3 4 5

3 LISTEN AND SAY. CIRCLE. TR: 10

4 LISTEN AND COLOR. SAY. TR: II

5 TRACE. DRAW AND SAY.

4 ANIMALS ON THE FARM

1 TRACE AND SAY.

2 LISTEN. CIRCLE THE ANIMALS. TR: 12

3 LISTEN AND SAY. CIRCLE. TR: 13

4 COUNT AND CIRCLE.

1 2 3 4 5 6 7

1 2 3 4 5 6 7

1 2 3 4 5 6 7

1 2 3 4 5 6 7

1 2 3 4 5 6 7

5 TRACE AND SAY.

REVIEW

1 MATCH AND SAY.

2 LISTEN AND SAY. MATCH. TR: 14

1 2 3 4 5 6 7

5 SHORTS AND SWEATERS

1 SAY AND MATCH.

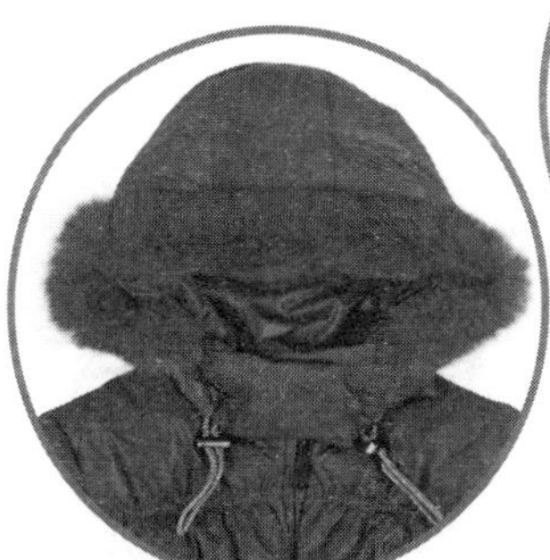

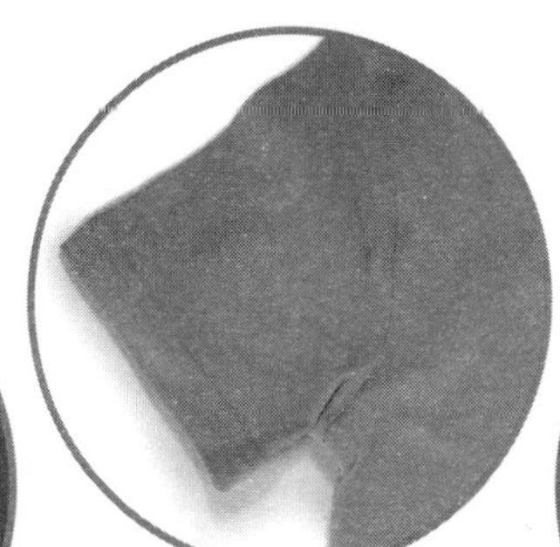

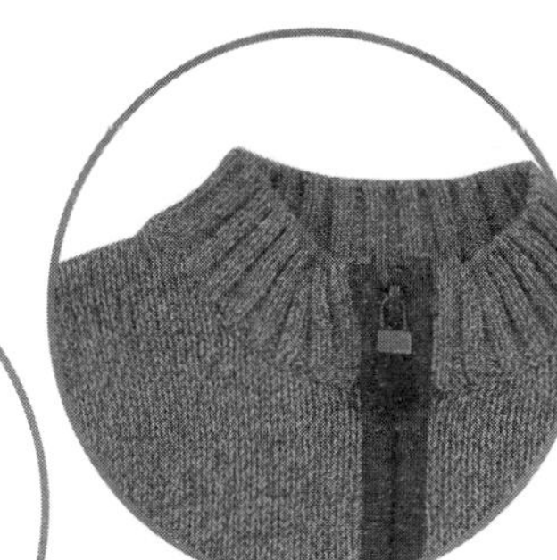

2 LISTEN AND CIRCLE. SAY AND COLOR. TR: 15

3 LISTEN AND SAY. CIRCLE. TR: 16

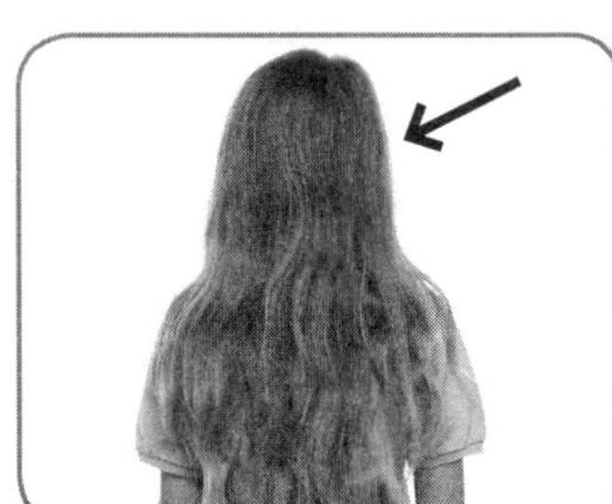

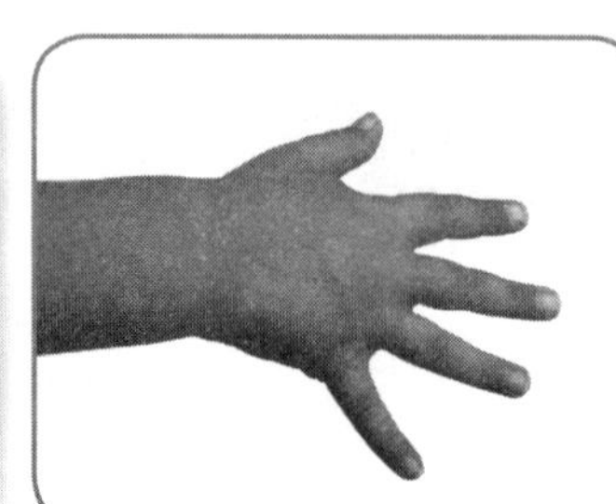

4 MATCH AND SAY.

5 TRACE AND DRAW. COLOR AND SAY.

6 I SEE A BEE

1 LOOK AND SAY. LISTEN AND CIRCLE. TR: 17

2 LISTEN AND CIRCLE. TR: 18

1

2

3

3 LISTEN AND SAY. CIRCLE. TR: 19

4 LISTEN AND COLOR. COUNT. TR: 20

5 COUNT AND DRAW. SAY AND COLOR.

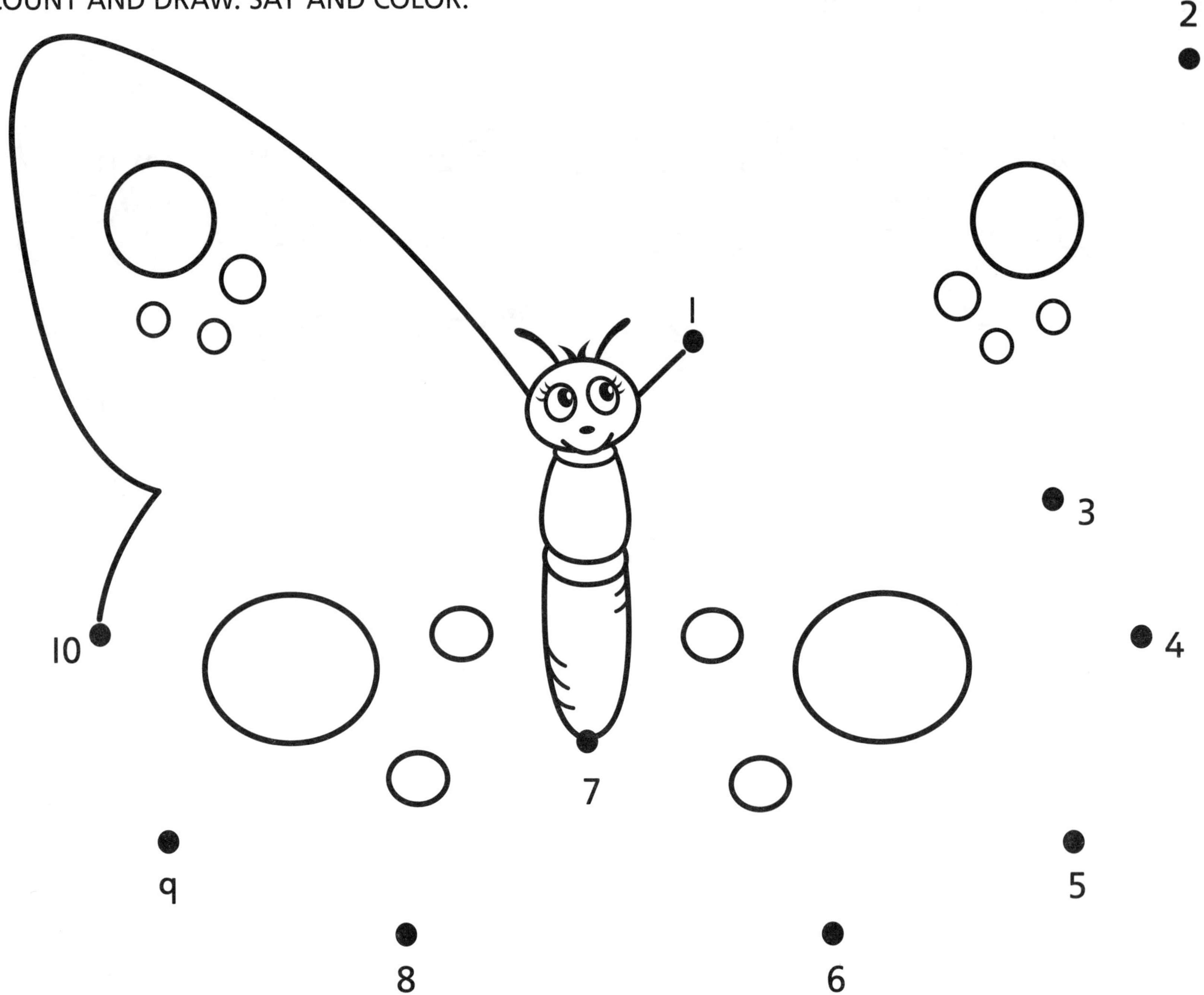

7 I'M HAPPY

1 SAY AND MATCH.

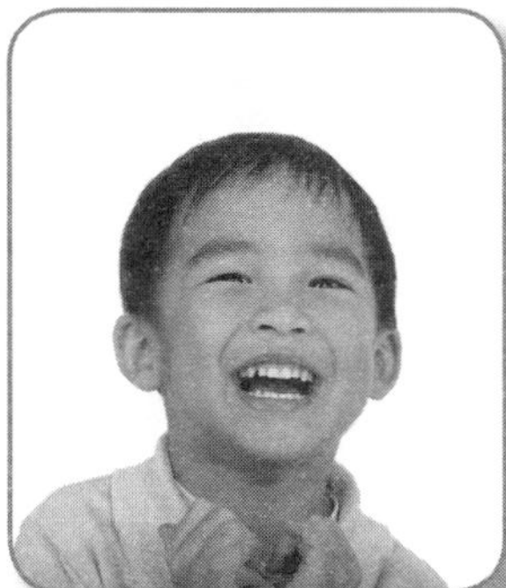
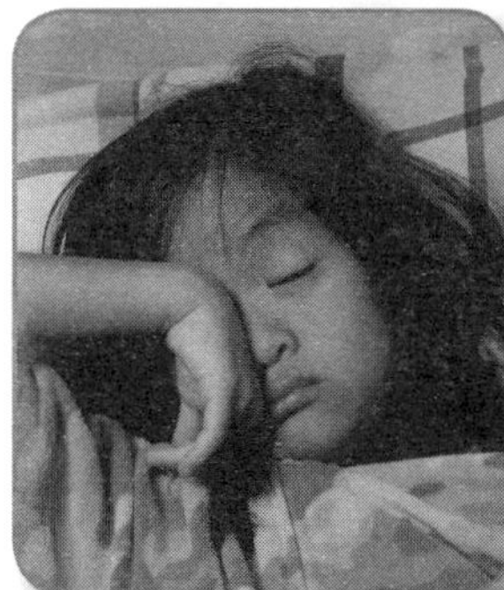

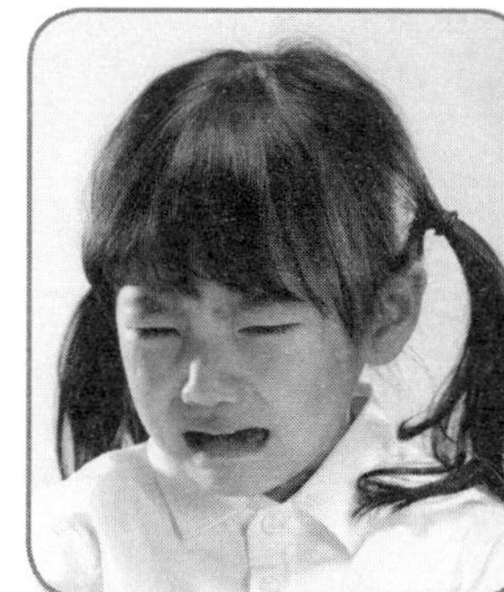
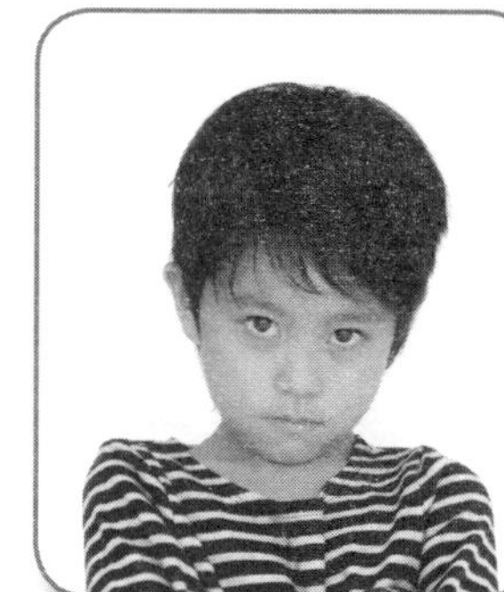

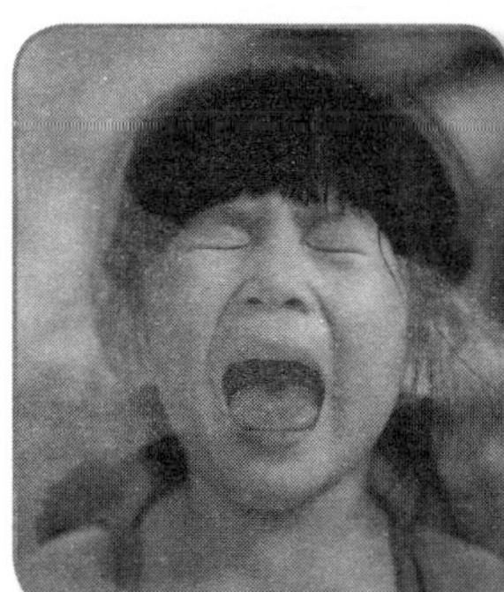

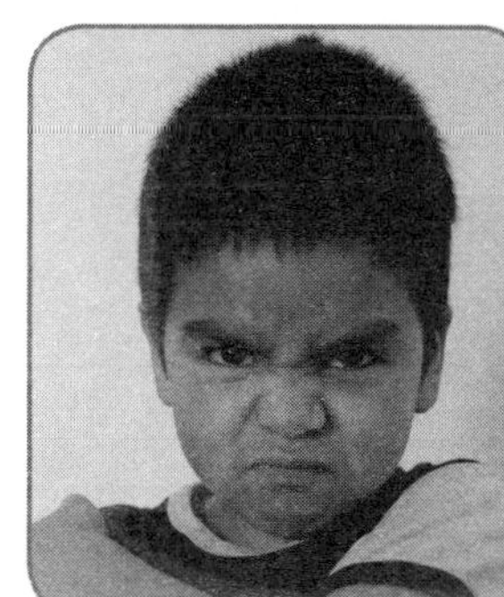
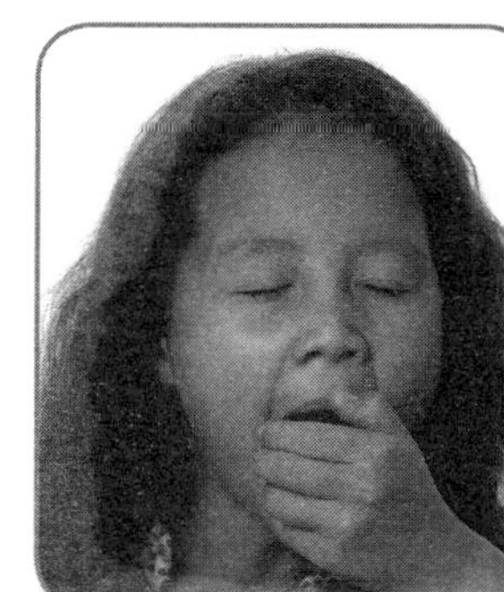

2 LISTEN AND CIRCLE. TR: 21

1

2

3 LISTEN AND SAY. CIRCLE. TR: 22

4 WHICH PICTURE IS DIFFERENT? CIRCLE.

5 TRACE AND DRAW. SAY.

8 BOATS, CARS, BIKES

1 LOOK AND SAY. LISTEN AND CIRCLE. TR: 23

2 LISTEN AND POINT. COLOR. TR: 24

3 LISTEN AND SAY. CIRCLE. TR: 25

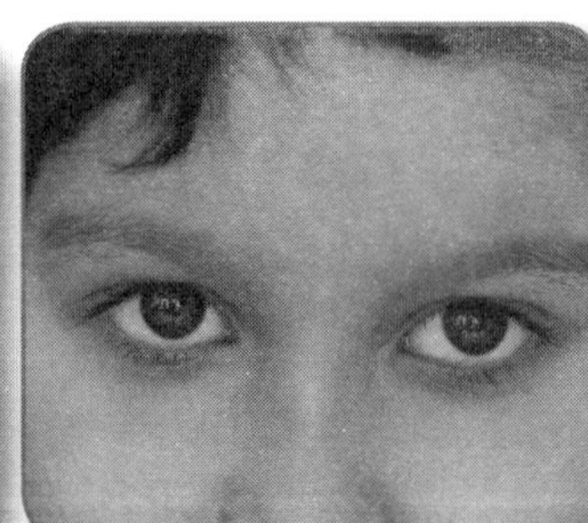

4 COLOR RED FOR *FAST*. COLOR BLUE FOR *SLOW*.

5 TRACE AND DRAW.

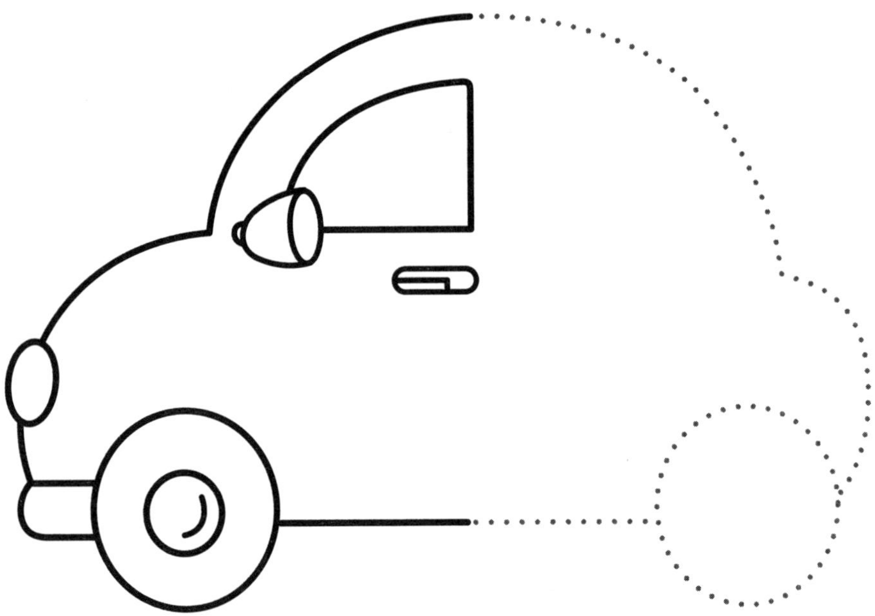

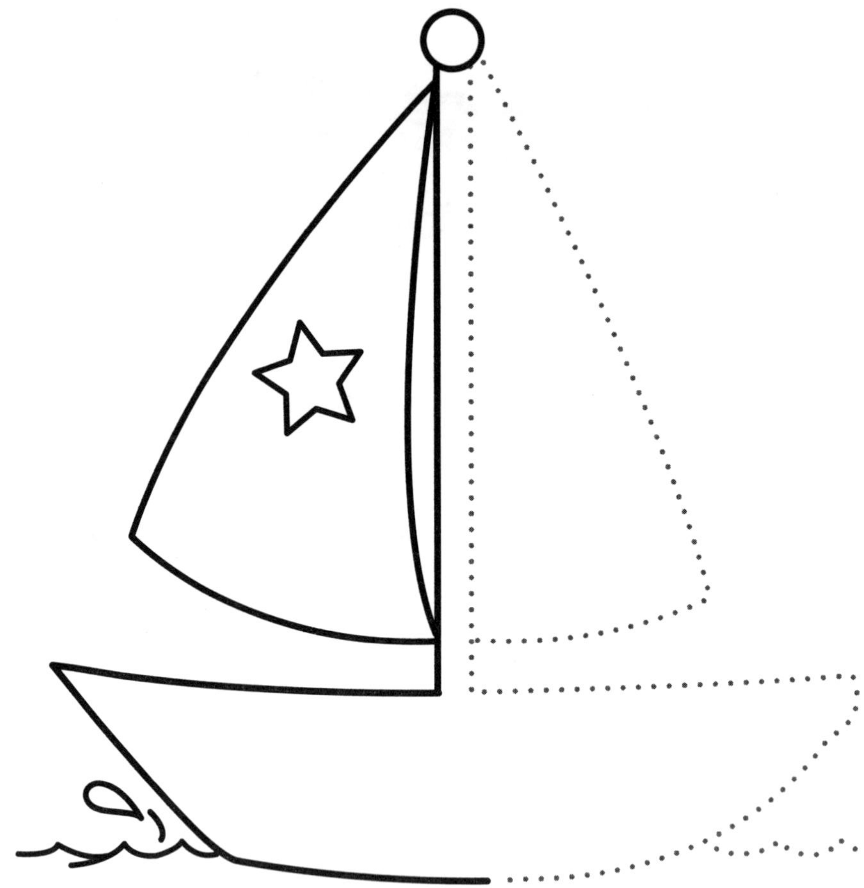

REVIEW

1 WHAT IS DIFFERENT? COLOR AND SAY.

2 LISTEN AND SAY. CIRCLE. TR: 26, 27

1 8 / 0

2  / 

3 10 / 9

4 8 / 9

5  / 

UNIT 1

LOOK AND FIND. COLOR AND SAY.

UNIT 2

COUNT AND SAY.

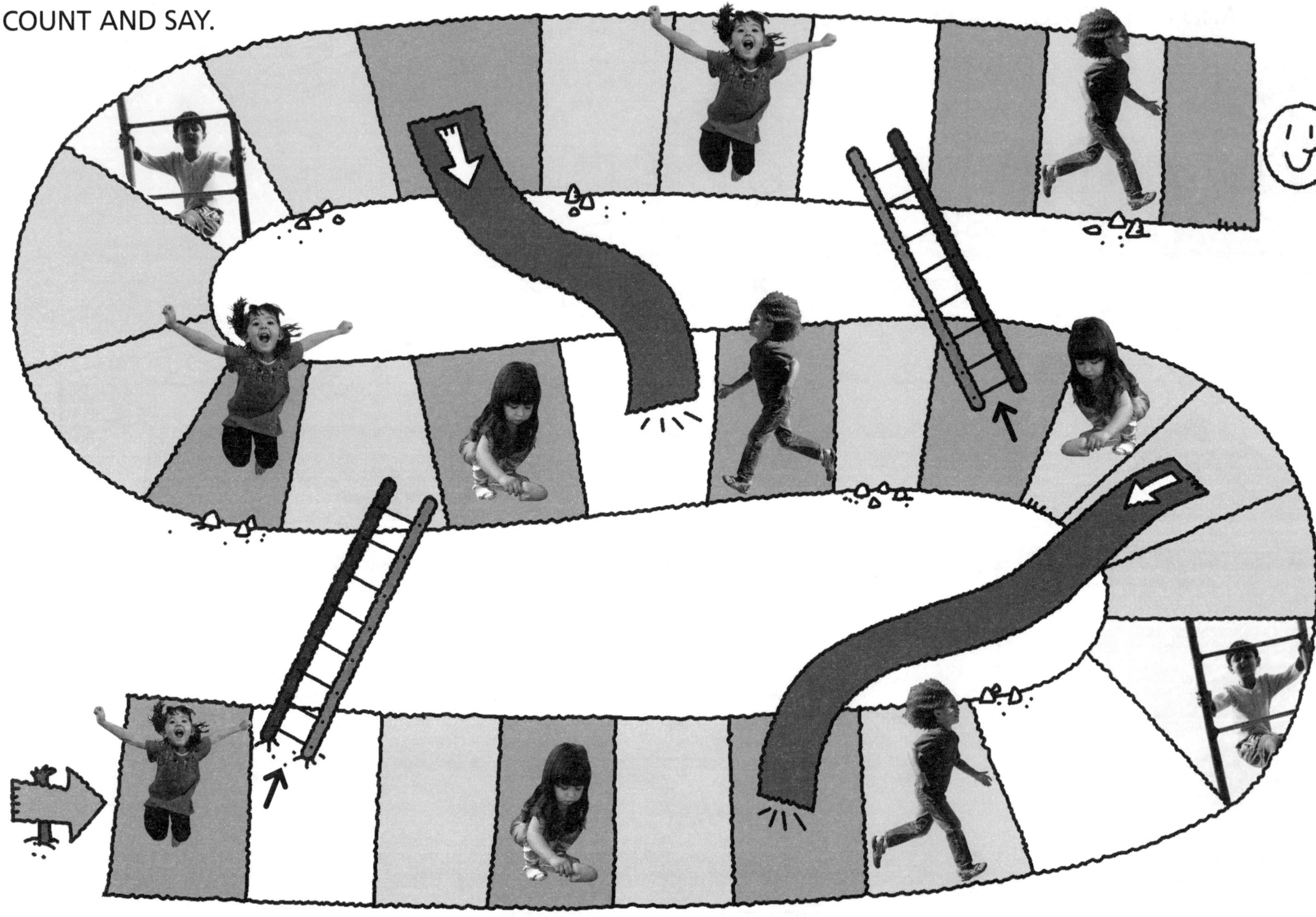

UNIT 3

LISTEN AND SAY. COLOR. TR: 28

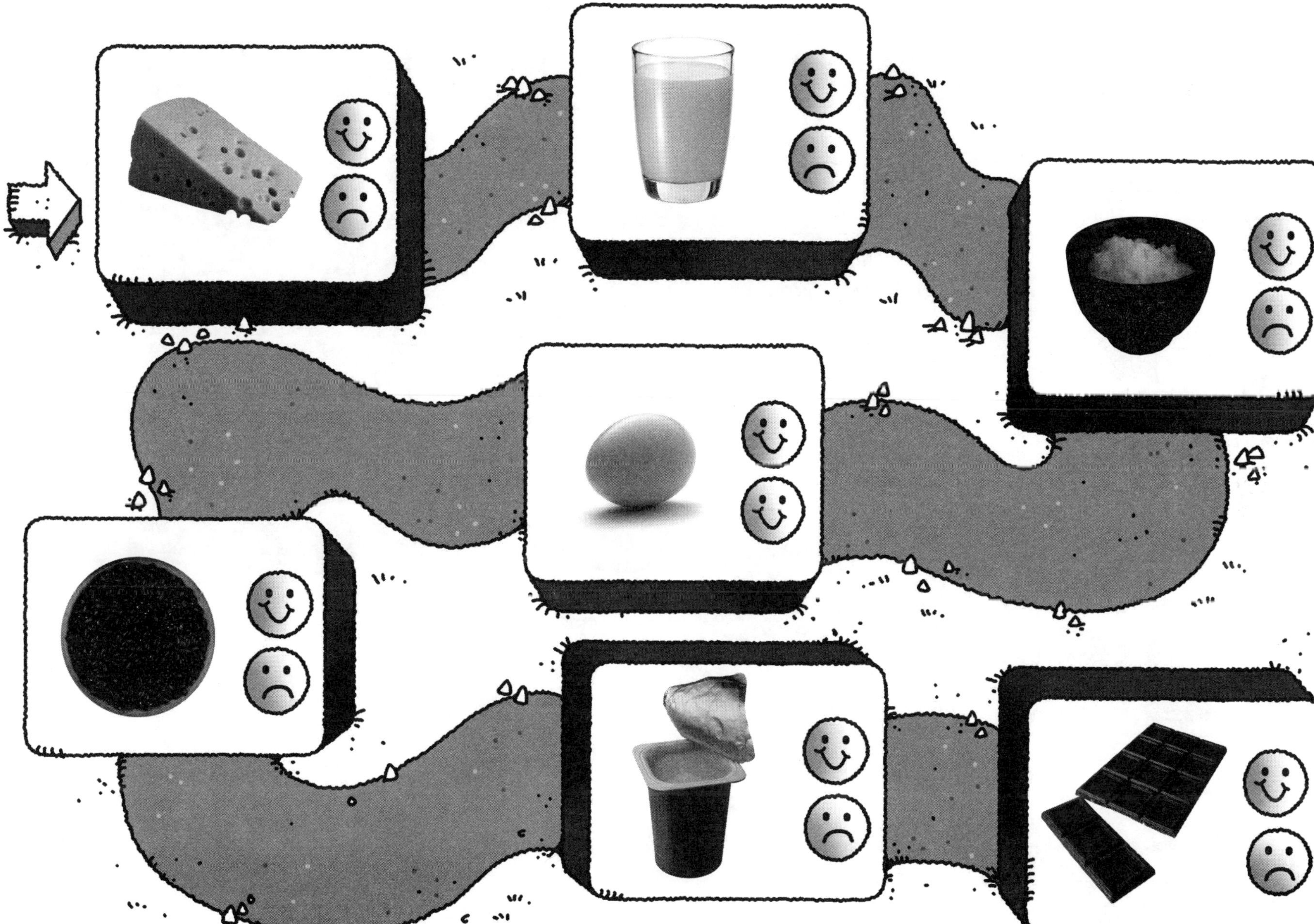

UNIT 4

LISTEN AND FIND. COUNT AND CIRCLE. TR: 29

UNIT 5

LISTEN AND FIND. COLOR. TR: 30

UNIT 6

SAY.

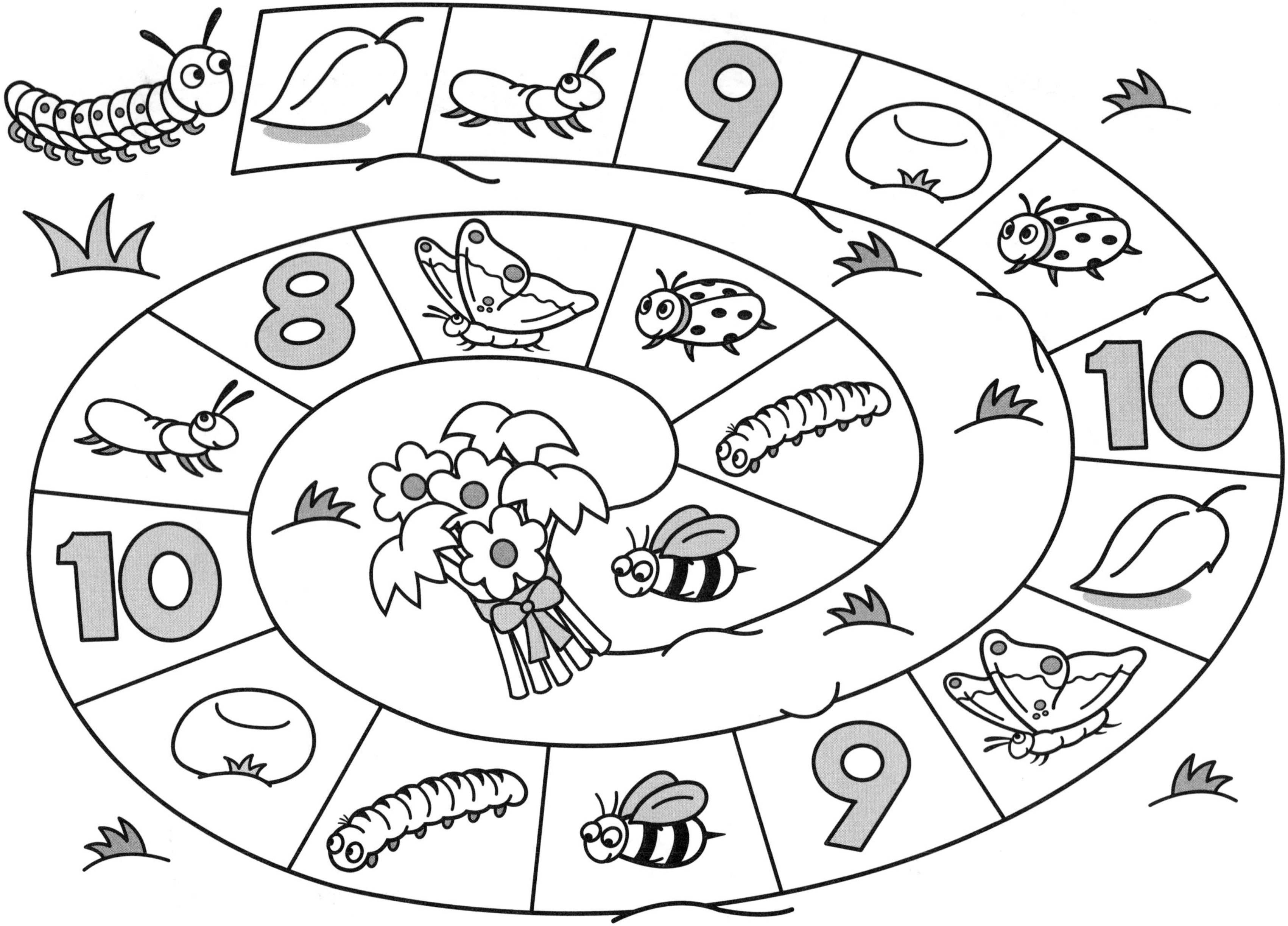

UNIT 7

LOOK AND SAY.

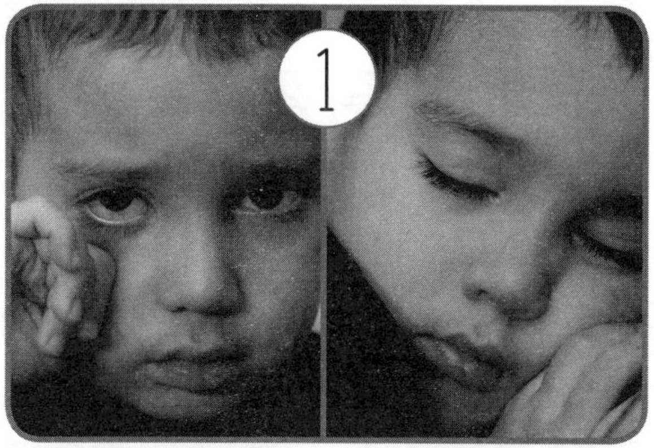

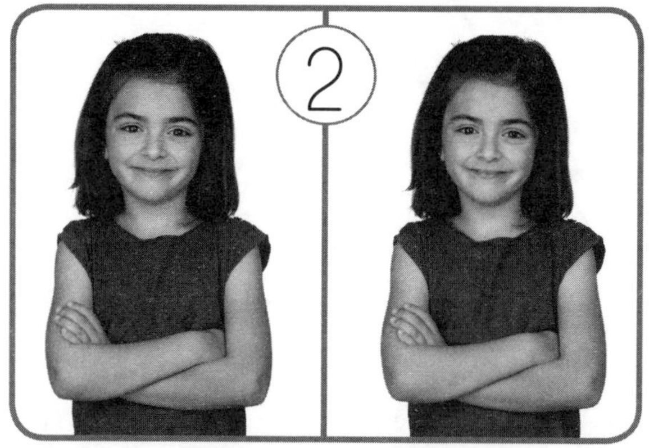

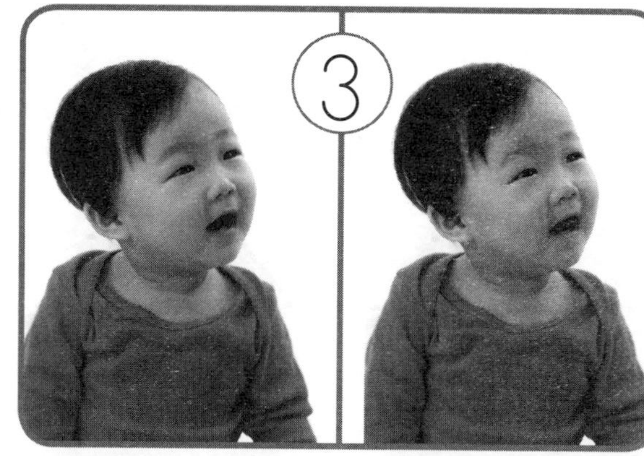

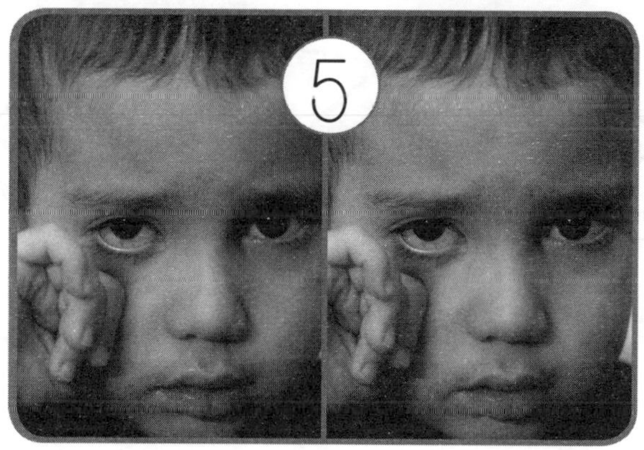

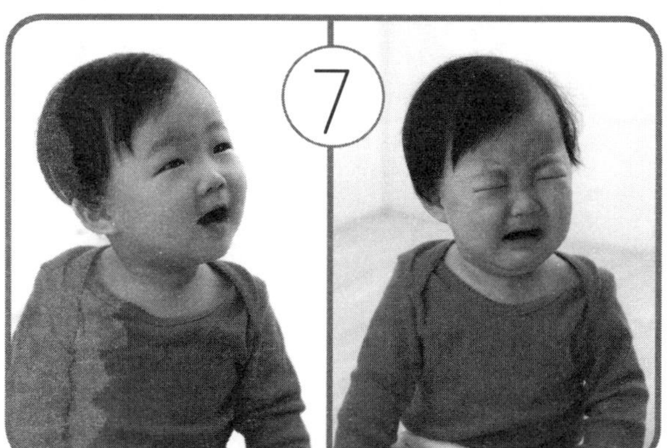

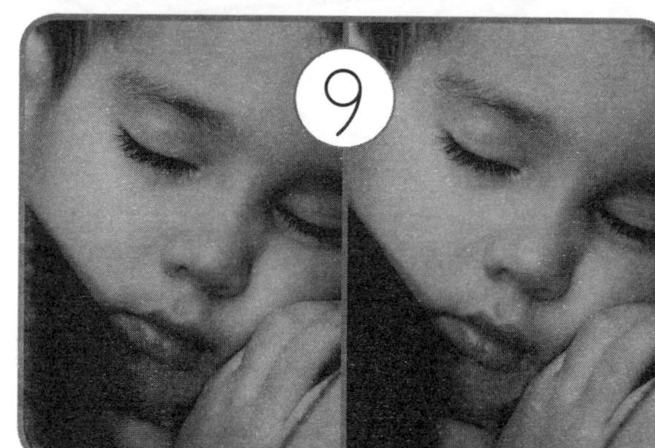

UNIT 8

LOOK AND SAY.

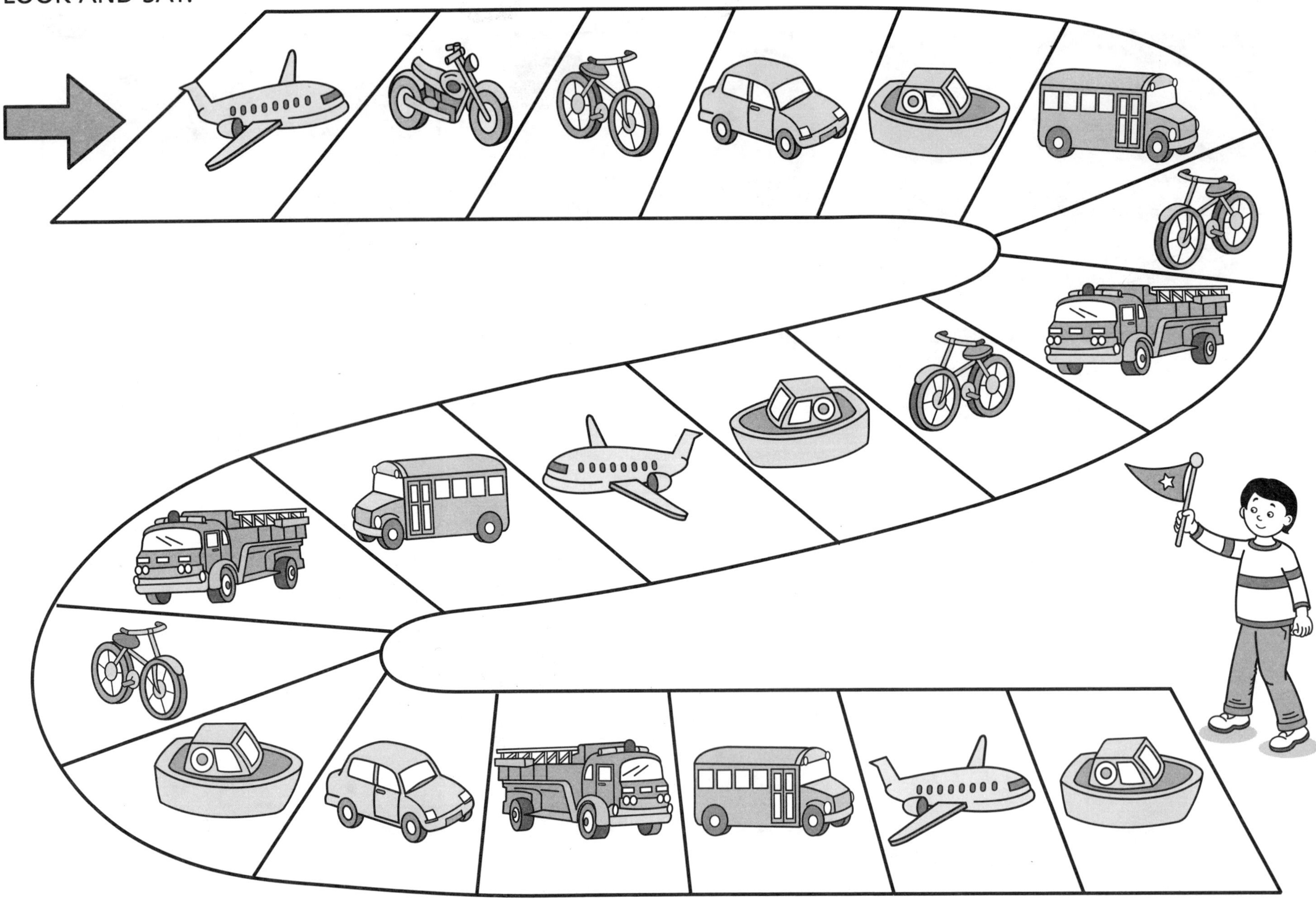